DATE: _____

FROM: _____

TO: _____

MESSAGE: _____

_____

First edition

2 4 6 8 10 9 7 5 3 1

Library of Congress Catalog Card Number: 99-61676
ISBN 0-7892-0602-1

Trust Yourself

Text by Helmut Walch
Photography by Andrew Cowin

ABBEVILLE PRESS PUBLISHERS
NEW YORK   LONDON   PARIS

When trouble comes knocking on your door, it's hard to believe anyone has ever had to overcome such obstacles. Remember—we all struggle with difficult situations, but if you trust in yourself, you'll have the strength to cope.

A fair-weather friend—and that's something I'll never be—is one who shrugs off your problems. But it's just as wrong to blow problems out of proportion. What's important is keeping things in perspective.

Fear is a poor advisor; you should always keep this in mind when you seek solutions to your problems. And of course it takes time to evaluate situations. Don't let fear become a constant companion.

Your dreams can become reality. You need only keep the faith and believe that you can make your dreams come true.

Fear of mishap often prevents us from doing things we want to do. But take a look at yourself: only he who is willing to take risks has the chance of winning. The passive one can never be the victor.

❧

Should there come a day when you're feeling down, one thing is for sure: you are a special creature. Your body and spirit—and the uniqueness of your soul—make up who you are. You should treasure yourself and you should stick up for yourself.

ॐ

You are the star performer in the play of your life. Try to fill your role to the best of your ability. That should be your most important concern. But if you can think first of your fellow players—that's the best part of all.

Don't expect others to come to your aid if you're not ready to help yourself. Others will stand up for you only as much as you are willing to stand up for yourself.

ॐ

The saying goes, "God helps those who help themselves." This means that he who forges his own way can also rely on the companionship and support of friends and family.

If you focus on your mistakes, you will sink into despair. Think instead of your individual strengths and reflect on how you can make the most of them.

Seek and maintain relationships with life-embracing people, because these relationships will mold you. It makes sense that you'll grow closer to those who also do you good.

What qualities must a tight-rope walker possess? He must be flexible and balanced. But what good would all that do him without self-trust? If he didn't have the courage to step out onto the rope?

Just think for a minute of the things you can do better than other people! No false modesty. And if you find yourself stumped, then you haven't really discovered all your many talents. Do it now!

Self-trust is by no means synonymous with arrogance. Others often have more trust in us than we have in ourselves. Just listen to them and you'll see that there's a reason why they place so much trust in you.

My wish for you is that one day doubt will become a stranger to you. That doesn't mean that you should become reckless. But courage and optimism can easily supplant doubt.

❧